Spring Bouquet: Poetry in Seasons

SPRING BOUQUET: POETRY IN SEASONS

First edition. 20th March, 2024.

Written by Emmanuel Borges-Da-Silva.

Table of Contents

If you are grateful for what the soil will give you, I promise you will grow.

a

I: Sunflower

Blooming 101

Life Vocation

Did you know that you've been a gardener since birth?

You came out with umbilical cord
and a shovel.

Where does the garden blossom?

Deep within your soul

You've been a gardener since birth

Tend to it. Tend to it. Tend to it...

Anthos Logia

We are much like the flowers
Here today and gone tomorrow
We long for refreshing
-as the flowers long for the rain's blessing.

Sunshine's pleasant for a time but we whine after
40 degrees in a concrete jungle feels like a disaster
But the beating hand of the sun marks the flowers in a special way
They grow from the heat and UV rays

Wind comes and wind goes.
And we are tested... As strong gusts try to pluck us from the pavement
We curse.
The flowers are inverse.
The flowers prove that their roots are too deep to be moved
... or that they may need to sink deeper into the ground.

The flowers use it all to grow
We complain and have nothing to show
We are more like creation than we know

"Grow today, be grateful.
there are more blessings
than there are disasters
focus on the growth"

Flowers in heaven

I wonder if they have flowers in heaven
I wonder if my brother took a stroll and plucked one
this morning
and breathed in glory.
For the pollen would be gold dust
The petals made of fresh air themselves

There probably aren't any flowers per say.
There needn't be

because all of God's loved ones are rooted in the clouds
and blooming for Him.
The people make heaven colourful, vibrant.

My brother is a flower in heaven.

„All along, you will see, you were blooming"

- Rhea Marcia

Hope has a scent

You smell like hope

when you water your own garden
trim your own bushes
till your own soil
feed your own cattle

... You smell a bit different

Hope has a scent
that fades with the pitter patter of rain
from the clouds above others' plains
their meadows are not made for your play.
If comparison is here, hope cannot stay.
How do you always find yourself over there?

You smell like hope

the more you practise
lavishing love on your own home
painting your barn walls with affection
and grace
and mercy

You smell like hope

though your land is not perfect
you smell like hope
when you learn to love it

"there is something
special and wholesome
about a person who
loves themselves, fully.
It spills into everything,
even the insecurity cracks
that reside in others.
With that being said,
there is nothing wrong with your life.
There is something wrong with your sight."

„Our deepest fear is not that we are inadequate. Our deepest fear is that we are powerful beyond measure. It is our light, not our darkness, that most frightens us. We ask ourselves, Who am I to be brilliant, gorgeous, talented, fabulous? Actually, who are you not to be? You are a child of God. Your playing small doesn't serve the world."

- Marianne Williamson

Fear of growth

People always talk about the fear of failure
But what about the fear of success?
When the lampshade comes off and your details are in full bloom,
shining bright for all to see;
strengths, weakness, insecurity.
Exposure is a terrorising thing... "what will they see when the light hits me"

Will they always be pleased?
Will I still bend my knee?
Will I stay submitted to authority?
What will happen to my humility?

Failing is not the only thing you should be afraid of.
Wilting like a dead flower and losing yourself to fame...
that should scare you.
Glancing in the mirror only to be met by a stranger...
that should scare you.

I am not saying that you should not shine your light
I am saying that you should be careful to know Who it comes from
It will keep you grounded when the fame comes
Hard work, smart work, gifts and talents... it's all grace.
There's no such thing as a man who's self-made.

Defibrillator

When was the last time you heard your own heartbeat
Laid on your own chest to see if you were still alive?

Flee to the fields
Only take Quiet with you

I hope you find God
I hope you find yourself.

II: Daffodil

Oh, to be pruned.

I see men like trees

A seed came.
Dropped into the soil of imperfection.

The seed grew.
Tall, into a tainted tree.

Fruit formed.
Internally rotten as sugar-bathed teeth.
Sweet-looking, inedible,
comparable to the prettiest bar of soap.

Anxiety wrapped in a smile
Depression wrapped in the guile of happiness
Trust issues wrapped in impulsive decisions
Fear wrapped in anger, wrapped in justification
... Fruit

Looks good but what's the truth?

Identity in upbringing
Identity in culture
Identity in race
Need for validation
Need for intimacy

... Root

To remove the tree and its rotten fruit
the axe of remembrance, acceptance... *repentance.*

This is the only weapon strong enough to yank this
tree from the soil

Oh, to start afresh.
The inception must first be addressed.
Hopefully this metaphor is simple and plain
Can a tree be born again?

"You were dropped into
a sea of filth before
you ever had the chance
of being a pure seed.
By being sown into this ground
you were always at an unfair advantage.
Our forefathers actions started
this unending snowball down the
eternal hillside that we reside,
but, God who dropped you into this soil
already made a way. You can be clean.
Just need to seek His face."

Wallowing Willow

We wallow as the willows
Hunched over and swaying to the dance of external forces.
Rooted to the ground you cannot escape.. Waking up day by day.
A curse for one, a blessing for another.
Another day of wallow or another day to finally change your posture.
Will you wallow in willow... will you be low forever?

"Perspective is everything friend sometimes, you just need to raise your head and look outside of you. You will see how blessed you really are."

Woven Labels

Who has the deed to your ears?
Who has the key to your heart?
Who is your designer?
... who named you?

Labels create cradles
For us to rest with ease...
You rest in the arms of who you believe
For it's their words you receive

There is a fight for your precious attention.

Who has the deed to your ears?
Who has the key to your heart?
Who is your designer?
... who named you?

Deep Rooted

The trees with the deepest roots last the longest.

Deep rooted trees are not taken by the breeze,

deep rooted people are not brought to their knees.

Darkness has no claim to these.

Decompose

Sometimes it's okay to waste away

to shed some skin

to spend yourself for the sake of others

If only you could see clearly

what happens to the soil

when you give yourself as a sacrifice

I know it feels like they have syphoned enough

but we all must contribute to this ecosystem

so that in due time others may glisten

Your turn will come soon

when others give all they are to you

but for now whilst you give

remember that through them, you live.

If you want to see a better garden

Don't only petition the gardener

In your community,

in your family,

in your corner of the world

I propose that you decompose.

"we grieve our own comfortability
before we even give it up.
we imagine, falsely, how bad
life will be if we give up something
for another... but,
once we get over ourselves
and embrace the death
of sacrificing our wants
for the needs of others
the lightbulb flickers on.
Ah... yes. It was always better to give
than to receive.
We have to get over ourselves."

For-Give

Offended
My drink was laced with justified bitterness
Unforgiveness launched a surprise attack
Because my heart was warm like sunshine and open as hungry mouths
... and they abused it.

It feels right to keep it.
But it is a sweet tasting poison.
They will be fine, but I will die in the end.
It's time to let go of pain.
Time to get out of the cage.
Time to for-*give* it away.
It's God's to take.
To live and love again, you must forgive today.

Don't give up.
This stage is the most vulnerable.
Because the biggest growth is just
around the corner.

A note for the future

You are growing.
You are opening up.
You are letting your beauty shine.

It took some time
But here you are
Enjoy it, you being alive

There will come a time
When you have grown enough
And your ceiling has been touched

You will be rewarded
With the shears of love
But it will hurt as your branches are plucked.

You will lose some things as you grow
Things you've grown to love
you will have to let go...
... eventually, another ceiling will be passed
And you will look back and see
That you have truly outgrown your past.

Isn't that what we do to plants?
We prune them so they can bear more fruit
Their existing frame cannot hold the growth to come.

"I used to wonder
"why do bad things happen
to good people?" or "why do bad things
happen when we are doing
everything right?" Are we being punished
or promoted? Are we losing or are we
being set up to grow? Observing
as many concepts of growth as possible
I have concluded, no growth comes
without loss or pain, whether it be
pruning plants, building muscle,
gaining better financial habits or learning
any new skill... something has to go.
You can rest assured knowing this...
You will gain more than what you
had to lose. Go and watch some pruning
videos. This is your Spring season.
This is growth."

III: Hēliotropion

Turn your petals to the sun

A Phenomenon

It was snowing in the beginning of March,
The day we collect the keys to our new home.
Where I come from, snow in March is abnormal
Likewise, ways in the wilderness, rivers in the desert.
Maybe God was doing a new thing
Was this a sign of the beginning of my new life?

It was snowing in the beginning of March,
The day we collect the keys to our new home.
The Spirit was dancing an odd but beautiful dance
through this phenomenon.
Oddly, it rarely snows in March
Beautifully, unique and bright, like our new beginning.
We had just buried mum

- the end of a chapter

Life had just begun

- the start of a "our happy ever after"

It was snowing in the beginning of March,
The day we collect the keys to our new home.
A new thing was happening, snowflakes poured from
God's throne.

"when change happens
and something new is delivered
we always have to grieve
a past reality
I wonder what new thing
is springing up in your life
that will exceed what you
are currently losing. Think on it"

The One behind the clouds

It was raining all morning
The lawn smiled and the birds retreated
"A good breakfast is always invited", said the grass to the bushes

In the conservatory I witnessed it all
In prayer I reached out to the God of this interaction.
The drenched garden shutdown the workout planned
But my eyes were enlightened
God was showing me something...

Where there is rain, sunshine must follow.
A cycle of provision from the lilies to the swallow.

As I sang to the Author of Creation
The sun rose and peered through the clouds...
Shining on my face, *intentionally*, for a moment
My heart heard, *"how much more will I provide for you?"*

I was being wooed.

"He can still be found,
the man behind the clouds.
He still wants to be found.
if you are quiet enough
nature itself will reveal Him"

A Promise

It was a difficult day of writing
The wind was crashing against my house
My mind was unfruitful and my fingers were numb from winter
Days finished early as the sun would sleep by 4pm
The last thing I wanted to do
was sit at a laptop and type
... nothing felt right

Until I looked up.
A gloomy day in December.
I observed dark clouds cover the heavens like a blanket...
If I could not look to the sky for my help,
where would it come from?

I was looking out of the window in my study
Out of distraction?
Out of curiosity?
I was caught by a glimmer in my periphery
An oasis in the desert, a luminary illusion; that's what rainbows are.
A cloud in the sky filled with all the colours of the spectrum that come from His white light.
The angle of visibility showed me
that this sign may have been just for me to see.

As quickly as it came, it went all the same.

I knew it was God.

This glimmer in my periphery gave me an epiphany
That my heavenly Father is always there behind the curtain
And though this world may be dark and gloomy, He most certainly is not
Nor is His love or His pursuit of human beings.

The floating mist of colour I saw today, were the flowers I never thought I needed.

In the Bible we are informed that rainbows are a sign of peace to us that God will never flood the Earth again because He found pleasure in Noah. I'm not here to debate the validity of the flood (though there is evidence), I write to give you hope. Aside from rainbows my Father in heaven gave a piece of Himself, His Son, the true "white light" for our cleansing and acceptance back into the holy family of God. I hope you see rainbows differently now and forever. I hope you see God's heart for what it is.

Days like this

Let's have more days like this
Where the clouds part like lips
The sun inspires endless photo clips
And our bodies move to the march of bliss

This beautiful communion marks the world outside
A type of vandalism that is far from a crime
Our widespread graffiti of laughter is painting the sky
Under open heavens may we come alive

Let's have more days like this
In heaven there will always be days like this.

IIII: Solidago

FLOWERS YOU NEVER THOUGHT YOU NEEDED.

LAWN'S WHISPER

Lay on me
Here you are safe
Though elegant and delicate
I can carry your weight

Lay on your front
With a book in your hand
Lifting your feet to the sky
Who knows where you'll land?

Rooted firm but wind-dancing
Come and sway with me
I have serenity to sell
I am grass so green

ONE DAY...

Creation is a reminder.
Creation is a mirror for us.
We will not be in cocoons forever.
One day, *we will be roommates with our dreams.*
One day, we will fly...

"if God was to encourage
the caterpillar who gazes upon
its future every time a butterfly
glides by, He would say
something like this; 'Caterpillar,
keep hoping for your butterfly days,
it will take time. Good wings take time,
good things take time...'.
human, you can remember this too.
good wings take time. Good things take time.
don't let hope go.

Spring Bouquet

I hope you will receive flowers
for all the seeds you sow
and the water you pour
on those who thirst for more.

Hope you will receive flowers
from friends and foes
for the light you keep
when darkness threatens to increase.

You will receive flowers
definitely,
even in death,
they flood us with their beauty
though we are not there to see it

Will you receive flowers?
For your next achievement
For pushing a baby out
For your new job
For baptism
For nothing... for just being here, maybe, one can hope.

Receive flowers
until they know longer make your cheeks strawberries,
your belly grow wings,
until you know you deserve them

for just being here and doing what you do
May flowers find you.

"Flowers
go, pluck them yourself,
for they are God's gift to us.
You are allowed to feel love
without waiting on another"

YESTERDAY AND TOMORROW

I'm starting to see that Spring is a "transition".
Spring is yesterday and tomorrow
For with it comes

the cold of winter
the heat of summer
the rain of autumn

An amalgamation of picnic dates, save the dates

If Spring is allowed to fluctuate, why not you?
Take stock of how you got here
Look at how much you've gone through

PROVERB 1 - NECESSARY

Who am I trying to impress?
What's impressive does not equal to progressive...

Overcompensation is the message,
How reflective!

It is obvious;
Glaringly,
That the impressive things you do are for the wrong muse...
Insecurity is the idol that your efforts go to...

Drink water
Be filled with goodness
Take a walk
Pour yourself into your purpose
Don't catch any if it overflows
Let it quench others' throats
Read a book
Grow forever, and ever
Spring clean your temple
You'll have more clarity than confusion
So much free space in your mental
Tell a joke at the right time
Laughter is medicine for the troubled... mind

...

What do you seek
-in this life,
is it peace?
Sorrow is for those who want to impress everyone they meet

Do what's necessary
Not what's impressive
If you want to be complete

Sow Your Seeds

Sow your seeds
And dream of leaves
That will shield you from the breeze.
Sow your seeds
And water the soil with the words you pray,
The garden you plant
Will feed you one day

The garden you plant
Will feed you one day

The garden you plant
Will feed you one day

THE REWARD YOU SEEK
IS IN WHAT YOU SOW AND WHAT YOU REAP

THE HARVEST YOU RECEIVE
IS THE REWARD OF WHAT YOU SOWED TO REAP

STOP LOOKING FOR YOURSELF

You weren't made to "*find yourself*"
Because you wouldn't know where to start... Who formed your beating heart?

...

He knows where to find you, even if you cannot find you.
It seems like your story is a constant cycle of ashes to beauty,
and maybe that's the point.
Maybe your life is showing others
that God really did make us from dust...
for without Him, you truly are.
... Depravity
starts at a molecular level and without the blood of Jesus that seeps down to our atoms there would be evil counted against you.

Eventually, your heart will emulate divinity
by entertaining an epiphany,
and with bright eyes know
you cannot save yourself
and that this is the best news ever
.
Humility is a gift to us, not a noble virtue.
Receive it, and let Him save you.

INSPIRATION

I am not like your parents
Nor is heaven akin to the home you grew up in
I don't want performers
Nor is there a place in heaven for such pride

Self-powered performance is but filthy rags in My eyes

I want lovers
And heaven yearns to be the incubator for this love
And the Kingdom, it's breeding ground

Final Remarks

Well done.

You made it to the end.

I have one last gift for you to

complete the bouquet.

The last offering

The gentle breeze and the calming rain
The slight sunshine and blooming plains
Here lay attributes that gives Spring fame
All these beauties come from one name

In the meadows, He is the dance and the sing
He was the first of all things but the last offering
Plucked from the fertile clouds; a King enthroned
Repotted on earth, to be harvested by His own

He is the bouquet sent from heaven above
... This was God's way of not giving up
God gave us flowers to show us His love
But we trampled His gift in our disgust

Although...

This was the plan all along
Trampled He was, He took on all of our wrongs.

Who is the Spring Bouquet?

The first of all things and the last offering
Jesus Christ, the Son of God.

He is the true bouquet of a bliss Spring
Receive Him. He is every good thing.

I have never grown tired
of smelling *this* flower.

"It's really easy.
Believe and confess
in your own way -
'Father and Jesus I welcome you
to live inside, bring
your Spirit too,
I want to eat with you...
Be my God'
Forgiven and adopted into the family.
The endless pit
of your internal longing,
satisfied.
His Spirit will change you.
No more fighting to be better
by your own efforts.
Supernatural self-help?
I guess so. This is the Gospel."

Acknowledgments

I want to say a big thank you to the First and the Last, the Yes and Amen, the King of kings and the Lord of lords, to my Father in heaven, Jesus Christ and the Holy Spirit for making this all possible. All glory and honour goes to God who strengthens my hands to write.

Shoutout to my biggest supporter, my wife. I am a better man because of you. I want to acknowledge my Mum, Dad and my brothers, as well as all of my cousins, uncles, aunties and grandparents. It takes a village to raise a child, so thank you.

I want to thank my pastors Ayokunu Oduniyi and Susan Deborahs Oduniyi for their support in my life. I also want to thank all of the other men and women that I may be forgetting for their availability to speak into my life and help me receive guidance when I needed it. I am growing into the summation of the puzzle pieces God placed in all of you. Thank you for your guidance.

Thank you, Jeffrey Osei-Bonsu, for getting me back into poetry and also helping to guide me. None of this may have been possible if it wasn't for your help.

And thank you to you, the one reading this book. My writings being valuable to you helps me to keep creating. Thank you and God bless you.

Fin.

About the Author

Emmanuel Borges-Da-Silva also known as Eman The Messenger is a content creator, fashion designer, poet, poetry script writer, emerging screenwriter, author and unique emerging voice who has several years experience doing commercial, live performance and online poetry/spoken word. Emmanuel has worked with notable organisations such as West Ham United Football Club, Finlandia University Women's Basketball (WBB) and various others.

He is passionate about using spoken word to ignite social justice campaigns, celebrate love (wedding performances), spread wholesome messages through music and much more. Emmanuel would describe his poetry as "poetic persuasion", which simply means to use spoken word poetry to poetically persuade people to change their perceptions for the better. Being a young carer for over 13 years prior to his mother's passing as well as his Christian faith-based background informs his love for change, growth, self-reflection and social justice for all.

Notable work includes, but is not limited to:
- Social Justice Campaign with West Ham United Football Club promoting unity within the football club against racism.
- Poetry script monologue for Finlandia University WBB in collaboration with Two Mile Media, encouraging the senior players on their season past and their season ahead as they leave the university.

- Poetry Album: The Black Tape
- Multiple bespoke wedding poetry bookings
- 8+ years experience performing live spoken word & poetry.

—---

www.emanthemessenger.com
www.linktr.ee/eman_the_messenger
Instagram: @eman_the_messenger

Business enquiries: info@emanthemessenger.com

Milton Keynes UK
Ingram Content Group UK Ltd.
UKHW041906120324
439302UK00005B/351

9 798224 800186